Recipe for
Teaching

To all reflective educators

Recipe for
Teaching

A
Reflective
Journal

Anita Moultrie Turner

CORWIN PRESS
A SAGE Company

For information:

Corwin Press
A SAGE Company
2455 Teller Road
Thousand Oaks, California 91320
www.corwinpress.com

SAGE Ltd.
1 Oliver's Yard
55 City Road
London EC1Y 1SP
United Kingdom

SAGE India Pvt. Ltd.
B 1/I 1 Mohan Cooperative
   Industrial Area
Mathura Road, New Delhi 110 044
India

SAGE Asia-Pacific Pte. Ltd.
33 Peking Street #02–01
Far East Square
Singapore 048763

Printed in the United States of America

Library of Congress Cataloging-in-Publication Data

Moultrie Turner, Anita.
  Recipe for teaching : a reflective journal / Anita Moultrie Turner.
      p. cm.
  Includes bibliographical references.
  ISBN 978-1-4129-5845-5 (pbk.)
  1. Teaching. 2. Teachers. I. Title.

  LB1025.3.M683 2009
  371.102–dc22

  2008034487

This book is printed on acid-free paper.

09 10 11 12 13 10 9 8 7 6 5 4 3 2 1

Acquisitions Editor:	Carol Chambers Collins
Editorial Assistant:	Brett Ory
Production Editor:	Appingo Publishing Services
Cover Designer:	Karine Hovsepian
Illustrator:	Mark S. Luckie

CONTENTS

ACKNOWLEDGMENTS

Corwin Press gratefully acknowledges the following reviewers for their contributions to this text:

Roxie R. Ahlbrecht, NBCT
Math Teacher Leader and Second-Grade Classroom Teacher
Robert Frost Elementary, Sioux Falls Public 49-5
Sioux Falls, SD

Patricia Bowman
Principal
C. Morely Sellery School
Gardena, CA

Linda Eisinger
Third- and Fourth-Grade Teacher
West Elementary
Jefferson City, MO

Lori L. Grossman
Instructional Coordinator
Houston Independent School District
Houston, TX

Mary Guerrette
Director of Special Education
Presque Isle, ME

Brenda Hood
Special Assistant
Washington State Office of Superintendent of Public Instruction
Olympia, WA

Carol Olney
Teacher/ Early Childhood Interventionist
Lambs Elementary School
Charleston, SC

Martin Scanlan
Professor of Educational Policy and Leadership
Marquette University
Milwaukee, WI

Tammy Angel Shiflett
Elementary K–5 Gifted Resource Teacher
C. A. Roberts Elementary, Paulding County Schools
Dallas, GA

ABOUT THE AUTHOR

Photo by Mark S. Luckie

Anita Moultrie Turner is an assistant principal of instruction at Charles R. Drew Middle School, and an adjunct professor at California State University at Los Angeles in the Charter College of Education, as well as being a much-sought-after motivational speaker. Her background includes classroom experience in the Los Angeles Public Schools; degrees in curriculum and instruction, human/child development, and special education for the deaf and hard of hearing; administrative and secondary teaching credentials; and staff development/teacher trainer experience. She has been recognized as Teacher of the Year (Crenshaw High School), Most Outstanding Teacher (Washington Prep High School), a Top Ten Educator in Los Angeles (Channel 11 News), a nominee for California Teacher of the Year, and an Emmy nominee for her work as coproducer of the Channel 58-KLCS instructional video series "Teachers and Their Coaches." Contact the author at www.harvest4succes.com

INTRODUCTION

Teaching is a noble, honorable, and challenging profession. The training to prepare to become a teacher requires years of preparation that includes college course work, student teaching, and successful completion of standardized tests. The training doesn't stop there. As soon as a teacher steps foot into a classroom, the life of a teacher continues in real-world experiences. No hard-working, diligent, and sincere teacher ever feels as though she has arrived. Each new year, each new school day, each new class, each new student brings new challenges and victories.

Robert Marzano, in the book titled *Classroom Instruction That Works* (2001), wrote: "After analyzing the achievement scores of more than 100,000 students across hundreds of schools, the conclusion shows that the most important factor affecting student learning is the *teacher*" (p. 3).

Even in these turbulent times, the teacher still has a profound impact on the success of his students. Despite other factors that seem to influence a child's daily performance, the teacher is an anchor that promotes the intellectual, emotional, and social skills of our youth.

Recipe for Teaching: A Reflective Journal is intended to be a companion to the text *Recipe for Great Teaching: 11 Essential Ingredients*. Each section is a reflective view of the ingredients discussed in the text. It also provides an opportunity for you to respond to the reflective questions at the end of each chapter.

It is clear that effective teachers are reflective about their practice. These teachers always consider how well they are doing with their students, how they can embellish what works well, what they could do differently in challenge areas, and whether they have effectively reached each child who crosses the threshold of their classrooms each day.

Recipe for Teaching: A Reflective Journal is intended to facilitate the process of being reflective about your practice. It will challenge you to look deeply into yourself, your students, your profession, and your ultimate impact in the lives of all those you touch: students, parents, colleagues, and community.

Finally, savor the activities in this *Recipe for Teaching: A Reflective Journal* as an opportunity for these ingredients to marinate and encourage your continued development in the profession. Teachers absolutely make the difference!

Passion and Compassion

The Power of a Great Teacher

SAVORY MORSEL

*There are two ways of spreading light: to be the candle
or the mirror that reflects it.*

—Edith Wharton

REFLECTION MENU

What are your reasons for becoming a teacher (other than money and benefits)?

_____

_____

_____

_____

How to your impressions about yourself (background, culture, religion, biases) influence your perceptions and treatment of students?

_____

_____

_____

_____

Why is love an absolutely essential ingredient for your effectiveness in the classroom?

_____

_____

_____

_____

_____

MIRROR, MIRROR ON THE WALL

Self-Reflection

Directions: List words or phrases that describe your strengths, abilities, or talents.

Make note of how these qualities or attributes can be maximized to promote your effectiveness in the classroom and encourage student achievement.

_____

_____

_____

_____

_____

_____

Self-Reflection

Directions: List words or phrases that describe your challenges, weaknesses, or limitations.

Consider how these challenges can be mediated so that they do not hinder your effectiveness as a teacher.

_____

_____

_____

_____

_____

_____

PERCEPTIONS

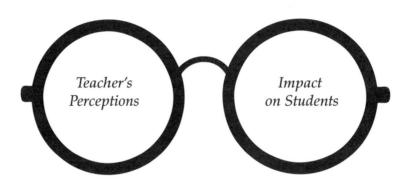

A Defining Question

How do you make sure all of your students learn when nearly 40% of U.S. citizens are racial or ethnic minorities who may see the world through a completely different cultural lens than you do?

—Bonnie Davis, in *How to Teach Students Who Don't Look Like You*

Directions: Consider how your own perceptions of your students might influence or impact the following:

- Interactions

- Expectations

- Instructional Practices

- Assessments

LOVE

Love is intense affection and warm feelings for another.

—American Heritage Dictionary

Others declare:

My love is deep, the more I give thee; the more I have, for both are infinite.

—Shakespeare

Love is the most durable power in the world.

—Martin Luther King, Jr.

One word frees us of all the weight and pain of life.

—Sophocles

Directions: Inside the heart, make a list that describes the things that you love in your personal life.

Reflective Morsel

Make sure to always stay connected to the things that you love. In a profession that requires so much of yourself, you must find ways to rejuvenate, replenish, and renew.

Take time in your day, week, or month to enjoy the things you love. It will help to keep you grounded in a sometimes chaotic and challenging life as a classroom teacher. Grading papers, calling parents, planning lessons will monopolize most of your time—if you let it. Take that bubble bath, vacation, long walk, or afternoon nap. It will make all the difference!

Describe ways that you show love toward your students.

_____

_____

_____

_____

_____

_____

Describe ways that you show a love for your profession.

_____

_____

_____

_____

_____

_____

Communication

An Essential Ingredient

SAVORY MORSEL

The bad teacher's words fall on his pupils like harsh rain; the good teacher's, as gently as the dew.

—Talmud

REFLECTION MENU

How do you encourage standard-English acquisition while maintaining the child's positive view of her first language?

_____

_____

_____

_____

Describe how you connect with students who come from a difference racial, cultural, or linguistic background.

_____

_____

_____

_____

How do you promote literacy in your classroom every day?

_____

_____

_____

_____

CONNECTIONS

List the ways that you connect with students from various backgrounds.

_____

_____

_____

_____

Definitions of Literacy

The ability to read or write. Having or showing extensive knowledge, learning, or culture.

Methods to Promote Literacy

Describe strategies that you use to promote literacy in your classroom (informal and formal).

_____

_____

_____

_____

Power of the Tongue

What you say matters! How you say it, really matters!

Directions: Take a closer look at your own ways of communicating with your students.

Note your responses to students (positive and negative) and words/statements that trigger those responses.

Choose your words wisely.

Consider a variety of conversations with students and your responses:

Triggers	Positive Responses
Student: This is a fun activity!	**Teacher:** Thanks. I worked very hard to prepare a great lesson for you all!
Your Turn:	**Your Turn:**
Student:	Teacher:
Student:	Teacher:
Student:	Teacher:
Student:	Teacher:
Student:	Teacher:
Student:	Teacher:

Triggers	Negative Responses
Student: This activity is boring!	**Teacher:** Be quiet and do the assignment anyway!
Your Turn:	**Your Turn:**
Student:	Teacher:
Student:	Teacher:
Student:	Teacher:
Student:	Teacher:
Student:	Teacher:
Student:	Teacher:
Student:	Teacher:
Student:	Teacher:

Cultural Interactions

Reflective Quote

Understanding connections between culture and communication is critical to improving inter-cultural interactions. The effects of communication skills are especially significant to improving the performance of underachieving ethnically different students.

—Geneva Gay, in *Culturally Responsive Teaching*

Reflective Questions

What are the positive words/statements that trigger positive responses from you or your students?

_____

_____

_____

_____

_____

What are the negative words/statements that trigger negative responses from you or your students?

_____

_____

_____

_____

_____

Are there any recognizable patterns in the trigger behaviors in your conversations?

_____

_____

_____

_____

_____

What changes will you make in your responses to these triggers?

_____

_____

_____

_____

_____

Describe ways that you communicate with your students to maximize positive outcomes.

_____

_____

_____

_____

_____

_____

Praise and Self-Esteem

A Spoonful of Honey

SAVORY MORSEL

All of us need to convey to our students and our colleagues every day that you are important to me as a person.

—Harry and Rosemary Wong, in
How to Be an Effective Teacher: First Days of School

REFLECTION MENU

How can you attach words of praise to specific tasks or activities that your students have completed?

_____

_____

_____

Consider the frequency of your praise to all of the children in your room: boys, girls, special needs, minority, gifted, talkative, truant.

_____

_____

_____

Describe how your learning environment exhibits evidence of equity, fairness, risk taking, and belonging.

_____

_____

_____

_____

KEEPING TRACK OF PRAISE

Directions: Consider the following questions as you reflect on the types of praise, the frequency of praise, and the students who receive your praise.

Before the Tally	After the Tally
How often do you praise your students?	How often do you praise your students?
Do you praise a particular student more than you praise others? A particular group/class of students more than others?	Do you praise a particular student more than you praise others? A particular group/class of students more than others?
Do you praise children who pose discipline challenges?	Do you praise children who pose discipline challenges?

Before the Tally	After the Tally
How do you build students' self-esteem?	How do you build students' self-esteem?
What types of praise do you use?	What types of praise do you use?
Do you praise a particular student, students, or class more than you praise others? Explain:	Do you praise a particular student, students, or class more than you praise others? Explain:
Does your type of praise change between particular students or classes? Explain:	Does your type of praise change between a particular student, students, or class? Explain:
Think about each face in your classroom. Do you offer praise to each one? Why or why not?	Think about each face in your classroom. Do you offer praise to each one? Why or why not?

SELF STUDY: PRAISE TALLY

Directions: Now that you have completed the reflective questions, complete this Praise Tally. After your findings, complete the reflective questions on the right.

	Monday	**Tuesday**	**Wednesday**	**Thursday**	**Friday**
Average Students					
Minority Students					
Defiant Students					
Special Needs Students					
Chronically Tardy or Truant Students					
Gifted or High-Performing Students					
Male Students					
Female Students					
Total					

Reflective Considerations

What did you discover about the areas of praise that were the same/different once you completed the tally?

_____

_____

_____

_____

_____

What adjustments in your professional practice do you deem necessary as a result of these discoveries?

_____

_____

_____

_____

_____

Reflective Quote

> _An effective teacher looks for opportunities to find people doing things right and knows how to praise those people so they'll keep doing things right._
>
> —Todd Whitaker, in _What Great Teachers Do Differently_

Reflective Morsel

After reviewing the tally, consider the frequency of praise for each group of students and increase the praise for underrepresented groups. Every child will benefit from praise!

Respect and Self-Respect

Marinating Positive Relationships

SAVORY MORSEL

Our looks play an important part in the construction of our attitude.

—John C. Maxwell, in
Attitude 101: What Every Leader Needs to Know

REFLECTION MENU

What types of social behaviors do you consider acceptable in your classroom?

_____

_____

_____

_____

How might you reinforce these skills in your classroom?

_____

_____

_____

_____

What role do you directly play to ensure that these behaviors are consistently displayed?

_____

_____

_____

_____

Reflective Questions

What do you consider appropriate attire when you go to work?

_____

_____

_____

_____

Describe the attire, etiquette, and communication among staff members on your campus.

_____

_____

_____

_____

Do you think that students are influenced by your daily attire? How?

_____

_____

_____

_____

POSITIVE FEEDBACK

Directions: Note the positive feedback you receive from colleagues, parents, or students regarding your demeanor, dress, and communication style.

Colleagues	Parents	Students

SOCIAL SKILLS

Directions: Describe ways in which you encourage students to develop positive social/behavior skills in your classroom.

Social Skills: Behavior	Social Skills: Communication

PROFESSIONAL ATTIRE

Directions: Draw a picture of appropriate attire for a teacher who seeks to be a strong role model for students.

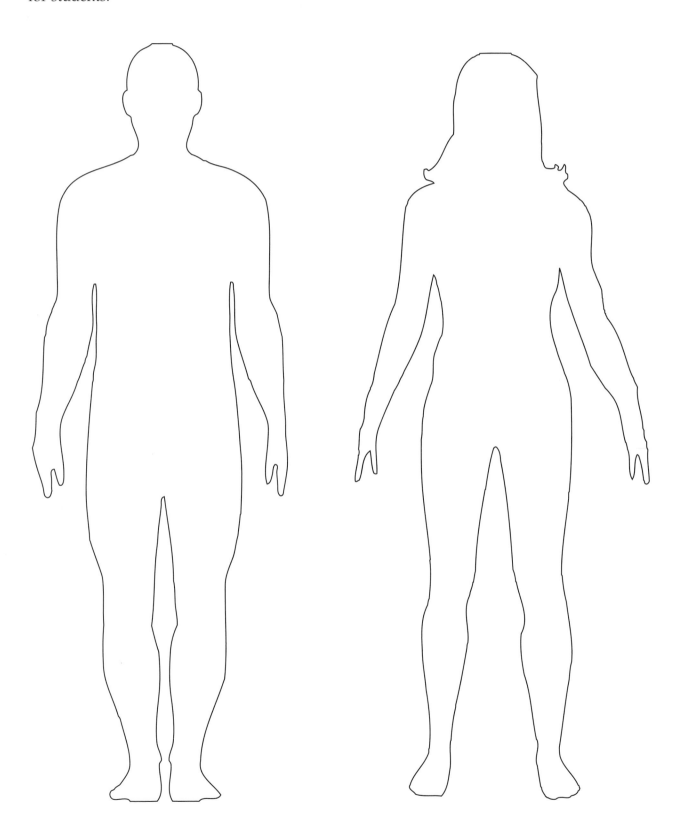

Reflective Morsel

Young people learn what is appropriate in society by looking at their adult role models. Your dress and your behavior are what young people will take to be appropriate.

—Harry and Rosemary Wong, in
How to Be an Effective Teacher: First Days of School

KEEPSAKE FOLDER

Maintain a keepsake folder that might include positive reminders of your great work as an educator, such as thank-you letters, notes, pictures, e-mails, merits, awards, certificates, and pictures.

Classroom Environment

An Equitable Dining Room

SAVORY MORSEL

Environment plays a critical role in the classroom. How you set up your room affects the learning that will take place. . . . Environment means more than the furniture arrangement.

—Moran, Stobbe, Baron, Miller, and Moir, in
*Keys to the Classroom: A Teacher's
Guide to the First Month of School*

REFLECTION MENU

How does your room's environment support learning for all of your students?

_____

_____

_____

Consider the variety of ways that student work is displayed in your classroom.

_____

_____

_____

How do you encourage your students to be excited about arriving in your classroom each day and considering themselves a viable member of the learning community?

_____

_____

_____

_____

Reflective Quote

A cluttered or barren room sends a negative message to your pupils. A well-organized, attractive room gives an "in control" image that students respect.

—Harry and Rosemary Wong, in
How to Be an Effective Teacher: First Days of School

LEARNING ENVIRONMENT

Draw an aerial picture (bird's-eye view) of your room's environment.

Student Work

Describe your strategy for displaying student work for a wide range of students (i.e., a variety of students throughout the school day).

Bulletin Board #1

Bulletin Board #2

Bulletin Board #3 or Walls

List the ways your school celebrates student work and student achievements throughout the campus.

_____

_____

_____

_____

_____

_____

ENGAGING PHYSICAL ENVIRONMENT

Reflect and document the following factors for creating an engaging physical environment.

What colors are used for the background on the bulletin boards?

_____

_____

_____

_____

What types of borders used around the perimeter of the bulletin board?

_____

_____

_____

_____

How does the student work show a variety and range of your students' skills?

_____

_____

_____

_____

How are depth, rigor, and critical thinking skills represented in the assignments on display?

_____

_____

_____

_____

_____

Is the student work authentic? Or did the students merely fill in a ditto or handout?

_____

_____

_____

_____

_____

Do the selections reflect a progression of improvement or exemplary/ anchor papers?

_____

_____

_____

_____

_____

Do you have a description of the assignment posted? Do you have a scoring guide or criteria chart posted with the student work?

_____

_____

_____

_____

How often do you change your bulletin boards? Why?

_____

_____

_____

_____

_____

Do you allow students to assist with the creation and setup of your learning environment? In what ways?

_____

_____

_____

_____

_____

How do you maximize the space in your room?

_____

_____

_____

_____

_____

Classroom Management

A Great Teacher Is a Master Chef

SAVORY MORSEL

Anything that you do not structure to your advantage, someone else will structure to their advantage.

—Fred Jones, in *Tools for Teaching*

REFLECTION MENU

What are the top five rules you think are important in your classroom?

1. _____

2. _____

3. _____

4. _____

5. _____

How clear are your procedures for creating an organized and well-run classroom?

_____

_____

What areas in classroom management need improvement? What changes will you make to ensure that these improvements are successfully executed?

_____

_____

_____

_____

_____

Reflective Quote

> *Classroom routines train students to carry out procedures with a minimum of wasted time.*

>   —Fred Jones, in *Tools for Teaching*

CLASSROOM RULES

Special Note: It is important to include your students in establishing the learning environment, that is, classroom rules, norms, bulletin boards, procedures, and routines.

Classroom Rules
1.
2.
3.
4.
5.

CLASSROOM PROCEDURES

Directions: Consider your procedures for a well-organized classroom.

Entering the Classroom
Leaving the Classroom
Submitting Classwork or Homework
Submitting Late Work
Responding to a Question
Sharpening a Pencil

Using Materials: Stapler, Hole Punch, Pens, Markers

Distributing Textbooks or Materials

Collecting Textbooks or Materials

Working in Cooperative Learning Groups

Taking Tests

Discipline

Making Sure the Cake Rises

SAVORY MORSEL

Many administrators are looking for teachers who can manage classrooms effectively, because they know that good learning can only take place when order and discipline are the rules rather than the exception.

—Rebecca Lynn Wilke, in *The First Days of Class: A Practical Guide for the Beginning Teacher*

REFLECTION MENU

How do you set guidelines for student behavior at the onset of the school year?

_____

_____

_____

_____

What measures do you use to ensure that standards for student behavior are upheld?

_____

_____

_____

_____

How do you effectively balance rules, rewards, and consequences?

_____

_____

_____

_____

Reflective Quote

Teachers who set and reinforce clear expectations for student behavior have more success in classroom control and fewer discipline problems than those who fail to do so. Effective teachers clearly communicate and reinforce behavioral expectations.

—James H. Stronge, in *Qualities of Effective Teachers*

FIRST WEEK OF SCHOOL

Directions: Describe how you start the first week of the school year/ semester. Specifically, describe verbal and nonverbal behaviors that establish effective classroom management, student discipline, and building of a learning community.

Day One

Day Two

Day Three

Day Four

Day Five

REWARDS AND CONSEQUENCES

Directions: Describe how you reward students for positive behavior/ work and consequences for negative behavior/work.

Consider whether you balance rewards with consequences. Teachers will get more buy-in by students if they feel that their productive behavior will receive more recognition than their unproductive behavior. Teachers must reward the best efforts of children and set boundaries/consequences for inappropriate behavior.

Rewards	Consequences

Organizational Skills

Celebrating Successful Recipes

SAVORY MORSEL

Success on any major scale requires you to accept responsibility. . . . In the final analysis, the only quality that all successful people have . . . is the ability to take on responsibility.

—Michael Korda, in benShea *Great Quotes to Inspire Great Teachers*

REFLECTION MENU

Why is it important for your students to learn organizational skills?

_____

_____

_____

_____

How does your classroom dynamic reflect your own organizational skills?

_____

_____

_____

_____

What other opportunities can you create in your class to teach organizational skills?

_____

_____

_____

_____

ORGANIZATIONAL STRATEGIES

Teacher's Organizational Strategies
Describe the methods you use to organize your own work and your classroom.
Students' Organizational Strategies
Describe the methods you use to help your students to organize themselves.

Reflective Morsel

A classroom teacher is the CEO of his learning environment. To establish and maintain a productive classroom, the teacher must plan and organize the procedures and routines used to maximize instructional time and provide accountability for students to keep an accurate collection of their work.

ORGANIZATIONAL SUGGESTIONS

Suggestions for the Teacher	Suggestions for the Students
• Maintain an electronic copy of the roll book with attendance and grades. • Maintain a hard copy of the roll book with attendance and grades. • Maintain lesson plans for the day, week, month, unit, etc. • Post an agenda on the board each day. • Require students to complete a warm up, dispatch, or bell work activity the first five to ten minutes of class. • Keep an enlarged version of the graded assignments on the assignment sheet. • Use crates, mailboxes, or trays to organize new or graded assignments. • Telephone parents or create an online classroom newsletter or blog. • Role model: Students will model your organizational skills.	• Take leadership opportunities to distribute papers, complete classroom duties. • Maintain an organized notebook, including assignments and grades/scores. • Keep track of homework by possibly using a student planner. • Arrive to class on time and write down the agenda or homework assignment in a designated place in the notebook. • Communicate with parents regarding progress in classes. • Maintain a line of communication with all teachers. • Choose a study buddy. • Complete class work/homework/projects on time and ask questions if an assignment is unclear.

Real-Life Skills

Cuisine for Life

SAVORY MORSEL

The mere imparting of information is not education. Above all things, the effort must result in making a man think and do for himself.

—Carter G. Woodson, in Bell, *Famous Black Quotes*

REFLECTION MENU

Can you list all of the real-life skills you need daily to live on your own? Your students need?

_____

_____

_____

_____

How do you reinforce real-life skills in your classroom?

_____

_____

_____

_____

Consider strategies to encourage parents to use these skills with their children at home.

_____

_____

_____

_____

REAL-LIFE SKILLS IN EVERYDAY PLACES

Consider the variety of skills that students can learn in everyday places.

Reflective Morsel

The standard for an exemplary instructional program is that it consists of rigor, relevance, and relationships.

Students will likely wonder how the assignments they are completing in your classroom benefit their everyday lives.

Directions: Complete this activity based upon the content area that you teach or the skills taught within that content area.

Document how you can embed real life skills into your subject area.

For example, what (math, English, science, social studies, reading, writing, critical thinking, organizational, listening, or speaking) skills can be used/applied in the library, at an amusement park, in the post office, and other places?

How can you incorporate these skills into your instructional program?

Library

Amusement Park

Post Office

Restaurant

Mass Transit

Grocery Store

Other

Reflective Quote

High motivation exists when students see the information or task as personally relevant.

—Robert Marzano, in *Classroom Instruction That Works: Research Based Strategies for Increasing Student Achievement*

The Whole Dinner

Collaboration and Equity

SAVORY MORSEL

Highly effective teachers possess the moral, intellectual, and social skills to use their leadership for good in the lives of students, parents, and colleagues.

—Elaine K. McEwan, in
10 Traits of Highly Effective Teachers

REFLECTION MENU

Describe the school culture on your campus. Are you actively involved in supporting the academic, social, or community programs at your school?

_____

_____

_____

_____

Do you have a homework hotline or newsletters accessible to parents to encourage their involvement at the school? In more than one language (when appropriate)?

_____

_____

_____

_____

Are you knowledgeable about the standards for the teaching profession in your state? How closely are your practices aligned to these standards?

_____

_____

_____

_____

Reflective Quote

The school's organizational arrangements and routines, attitudes and beliefs, and the relationships among everyone in the building shape what students accomplish in school.

—Jeannie Oaks and Martin Lipton, in *Teaching to Change the World*

VISION STATEMENT

Name of Your School _____

Directions: Write the school's *vision statement*.

_____

_____

_____

_____

MISSION STATEMENT

Name of Your School _____

Directions: Write the school's *mission statement*.

_____

_____

_____

_____

ACADEMIC, SOCIAL, AND COMMUNITY ACTIVITIES

Directions: Document the academic, social, and community activities that occur at your school to encourage connections among all stakeholders.

Academic Activities	Social Activities	Community Activities

CLASSROOM AND SCHOOL NEWSLETTERS

Does your school have a monthly newsletter or other type of publication (hard copy or electronic)? Describe its impact or influence on your school community.

_____

_____

_____

Do you have a classroom newsletter or other type of publication (hard copy or electronic)? Describe its impact or influence on your school community.

_____

_____

_____

IT TAKES A VILLAGE: PARENTAL INVOLVEMENT

"It takes a village to raise a child."

Describe the strategies you use to encourage parental support and involvement in your instructional program.

_____

_____

_____

_____

_____

Describe the strategies you use to encourage community support and involvement in your instructional program.

_____

_____

_____

_____

_____

LET'S TAKE A CLOSER LOOK

Directions: Describe specific evidence that your own instructional program/teaching practices support the vision and mission of your school.

Evidence #1

Activity:

Impact:

Evidence #2

Activity:

Impact:

Evidence #3

Activity:

Impact:

Evidence #4

Activity:

Impact:

Evidence #5

Activity:

Impact:

Keep a teacher portfolio of your great ideas, strategies, and activities!

Welcome to the Table

SAVORY MORSEL

A teacher affects eternity; he can never tell where his influence stops.

—Henry Adams, in Davidoff,
The Pocket Book of Quotations

REFLECTION MENU

How do you see your profession as more than just a job to get
a paycheck?

_____

_____

_____

_____

In what ways do you create foundations that promote lifelong successes
for your students?

_____

_____

_____

_____

How will your academic feast be embellished now that you have read this text?

_____

_____

_____

_____

CELEBRATE YOUR CLASSROOM

Directions: Describe successful strategies and techniques you use in your own classroom.

Strategy	Student Evidence

3-2-1 REFLECTION

3 Things I Learned From Reading This Book:

2 Things I Can Use Immediately in My Own Classroom:

1 Thing in My Teaching Practice That Needs More Work:

REFLECTIVE JOURNAL WRITING: TRUE STORIES

Directions: Each day brings new rewards, challenges, and noteworthy examples of success. Document your own real-life examples and celebrate them with your colleagues, parents, and students. Enjoy!

True Story #1:

True Story #2:

True Story #3:

True Story #4:

True Story #5:

True Story #6:

True Story #7:

True Story #8:

True Story #9:

True Story #10:

Request to Teachers: Please submit one of your own "True Stories" at www.harvest4success.com.

PROFESSIONAL/PERSONAL CONTACTS

Name	Address	Telephone	E-Mail

NOTES

NEXT STEPS

Directions: Describe the ways in which you will change, embellish, or strengthen your professional practice.

1. _____

_____

2. _____

_____

3. _____

_____

4. _____

_____

5. _____

_____

Every ingredient that has been addressed in *Recipe for Teaching: A Reflective Journal*, if measured out with careful considerations, can contribute to a rigorous, challenging, and relevant learning environment leading to your students' academic achievement and your own personal growth as an effective teacher.

The greatest and most powerful people in our world sat in a teacher's classroom!

You are awesome!

REFERENCES

Bell, J. C. (1995). *Famous black quotations* (p. 109). New York: Warner Books.

benShea, N. (2002). *Great quotes to inspire great teachers* (pp. 59, 137). Thousand Oaks, CA: Corwin Press.

Davidoff, H. (1952). *The pocket book of quotations* (p. 391). New York: Pocket Books.

Davies, P. (1972). *American Heritage Dictionary* (p. 530). Boston: Houghton Mifflin.

Davis, B. M. (2007). *How to teach students who don't look like you: Culturally relevant teaching strategies*. Thousand Oaks, CA: Corwin Press.

Gay, G. (2000). *Culturally responsive teaching: Theory, research & practice*. New York: Teachers College Press.

Jones, F. (2007). *Tools for teaching*. Santa Cruz, CA: Fredric H. Jones & Associates, Inc.

Marzano, R., Pickering, D., & Pollock, J. (2001). *Classroom instruction that works: Research-based strategies for increasing student achievement*. Richmond, VA: Association for Supervision and Curriculum Development.

Maxwell, J. C. (2003). *Attitude 101: What every leader needs to know*. Nashville, TN: Thomas Nelson.

McEwan, E. K. (2002). *10 traits of highly effective teachers*. Thousand Oaks, CA: Corwin Press.

Moran, C., Stobbe, J., Baron, W., Miller, J., & Moir, E. (2000). *Keys to the classroom: A teacher's guide to the first month of school* (2nd ed.). Thousand Oaks, CA: Corwin Press.

Oakes, J., & Lipton, M. (2007). *Teaching to change the world*. New York: McGraw-Hill.

Stronge, J. H. (2002). *Qualities of effective teachers*. Alexandria, VA: Association for Supervision and Curriculum Development.

Tileston, D. W. (2004). *What every teacher should know about student motivation*. Thousand Oaks, CA: Corwin Press.

Whitaker, T. (2004). *What great teachers do differently*. Larchmont, NY: Eye On Education, Inc.

Wilke, R. L. (2003). *The first days of class: A practical guide for the beginning teacher*. Thousand Oaks, CA: Corwin Press.

Wong, H. K., & Wong, R. T. (2005). *How to be an effective teacher: First days of school*. Mountain View, CA: Harry K. Wong Publications, Inc.

The Corwin Press logo—a raven striding across an open book—represents the union of courage and learning. Corwin Press is committed to improving education for all learners by publishing books and other professional development resources for those serving the field of PreK–12 education. By providing practical, hands-on materials, Corwin Press continues to carry out the promise of its motto: **"Helping Educators Do Their Work Better."**

Work Place Guide 4B Measuring in Yards

Summary

Students work in pairs to choose objects in and near the classroom to measure in yards. First, they find an object to measure and write the name of the object on their record sheets. Then they estimate the length of the object, and finally measure it to the nearest yard, using a yard-long piece of string.

Skills & Concepts

- Measure the length of an object in yards (2.MD.1)
- Estimate length in yards (2.MD.3)
- Measure length to the nearest whole unit in customary units (supports 2.MD)

Materials

Copies	Kit Materials	Classroom Materials
TM T1 Work Place Guide 4B Measuring in Yards **TM T2** Work Place Instructions 4B Measuring in Yards **TM T3** 4B Measuring in Yards Record Sheet		· 1-yard lengths of heavy cotton string (3)

Assessment & Differentiation

Here are some quick observational assessments you can make as students begin to play this game on their own. Use the results to differentiate as needed.

If you see that...	Differentiate	Example
Students are having trouble measuring lengths longer than a yard with the string.	**SUPPORT** Remind students of the measuring techniques discussed in class.	Students can work together to stretch out the string, hold it down on one end, and then move the other end around to measure a second yard.
Students are having a hard time finding appropriate items to measure.	**SUPPORT** Show students how to measure one appropriate item in the room and then challenge them to find other objects around the room that are similar in length, or longer than, the first object. You might also have an adult helper take small groups of students to locations around the school that might have objects suitable for measuring in yards, such as the gym, the cafeteria, and/or the playground.	Have students estimate and measure the height of the classroom door, and then find other objects around the room that are at least as long as the door is high.
Students are having a hard time measuring to the nearest whole yard.	**SUPPORT** If this problem comes up during Work Places, you may want to discuss it with the entire class. First, solicit and try suggestions from the students. Then if it doesn't come from the class, show students how to fold a yard-string in half and mark it at the half-way point with a small piece of masking tape. Then show them that when an object doesn't measure an exact number of whole yards, they can look to see whether the "final bit" falls before the half-way mark, exactly at the half-way mark, or after the half-way mark.	If an object measures 3 yards and some more, look to see if the "some more" is less than half, exactly half, or more than half a yard. If it is less than a half, it is 3 yards if measured to the nearest yard. If it is more than a half, it is 4 yards if measured to the nearest yard. If it falls exactly at the half-way mark, students can be encouraged to record 3 ½, or 3 and a half.
One or more students are working quickly and successfully to complete the sheet.	**CHALLENGE** Have students find pairs of objects for each line of the sheet. The pairs of objects should be as close to the same length as possible.	Clever students may list "left side of the door" and "right side of the door" as a potential pair.

T1

Instrucciones de Work Place 4B Medir en yardas

1   Cada estudiante necesita una hoja de anotaciones y un lápiz. Las parejas de estudiantes comparten una cuerda de una yarda de longitud.

2   Cada compañero estima cuán largo es el objeto en yardas y anota su estimación en su hoja de anotaciones. (Las estimaciones de los compañeros no tienen que coincidir).

3   Los compañeros se ayudan entre sí para medir el objeto a la yarda entera más próxima, usando la cuerda de una yarda de longitud.

4   Los compañeros repiten cada uno de los pasos anteriores hasta que hayan completado sus hojas de anotaciones.

Unit 4 Module 2 | Session 2 *class set, plus more as needed, stored in the Work Place bin*

NOMBRE Xavier | FECHA

4B Medir en yardas — Hoja de anotaciones

Usa tu cuerda de yarda para estimar y medir la longitud en yardas.

- Elige lo que desees medir. Escríbelo en tu hoja de anotaciones.
- Registra tu estimación. ¿Cuántas yardas de largo crees que tiene?
  Haz esto antes de medir.
- Mide la longitud a la yarda más cercana usando la cuerda de yarda.

Mi objeto	Mi estimación	Longitud real
a La altura del Sr. Frisby	2 yardas	2 yardas
b	_____ yardas	_____ yardas
c	_____ yardas	_____ yardas
d	_____ yardas	_____ yardas
e	_____ yardas	_____ yardas
f	_____ yardas	_____ yardas

Bridges in Mathematics Grade 2 Teacher Masters   T3   © The Math Learning Center | mathlearningcenter.org

---

Work Place Guide 4B Measuring in Yards

Summary

Students work in pairs to choose objects in and near the classroom to measure in yards. First, they find an object to measure and write the name of the object on their record sheets. Then they estimate the length of the object, and finally measure it to the nearest yard, using a yard-long piece of string.

Skills & Concepts

- Measure the length of an object in yards (2.MD.1)
- Estimate length in yards (2.MD.3)
- Measure length to the nearest whole unit in customary units (supports 2.MD)

Materials

Copies	Kit Materials	Classroom Materials
TM T1 Work Place Guide 4B Measuring in Yards **TM T2** Work Place Instructions 4B Measuring in Yards **TM T3** 4B Measuring in Yards Record Sheet		• 1-yard lengths of heavy cotton string (3)

Assessment & Differentiation

Here are some quick observational assessments you can make as students begin to play this game on their own. Use the results to differentiate as needed.

If you see that...	Differentiate	Example
Students are having trouble measuring lengths longer than a yard with the string.	**SUPPORT** Remind students of the measuring techniques discussed in class.	Students can work together to stretch out the string, hold it down on one end, and then move the other end around to measure a second yard.
Students are having a hard time finding appropriate items to measure.	**SUPPORT** Show students how to measure one appropriate item in the room and then challenge them to find other objects around the room that are similar in length, or longer than, the first object. You might also have an adult helper take small groups of students to locations around the school that might have objects suitable for measuring in yards, such as the gym, the cafeteria, and/or the playground.	Have students estimate and measure the height of the classroom door, and then find other objects around the room that are at least as long as the door is high.
Students are having a hard time measuring to the nearest whole yard.	**SUPPORT** If this problem comes up during Work Places, you may want to discuss it with the entire class. First, solicit and try suggestions from the students. Then if it doesn't come from the class, show students how to fold a yard-string in half and mark it at the half-way point with a small piece of masking tape. Then show them that when an object doesn't measure an exact number of whole yards, they can look to see whether the "final bit" falls before the half-way mark, exactly at the half-way mark, or after the half-way mark.	If an object measures 3 yards and some more, look to see if the "some more" is less than half, exactly half, or more than half a yard. If it is less than a half, it is 3 yards if measured to the nearest yard. If it is more than a half, it is 4 yards if measured to the nearest yard. If it falls exactly at the half-way mark, students can be encouraged to record 3 ½, or 3 and a half.
One or more students are working quickly and successfully to complete the sheet.	**CHALLENGE** Have students find pairs of objects for each line of the sheet. The pairs of objects should be as close to the same length as possible.	Clever students may list "left side of the door" and "right side of the door" as a potential pair.

T1

Instrucciones de Work Place 4B Medir en yardas

1 Cada estudiante necesita una hoja de anotaciones y un lápiz. Las parejas de estudiantes comparten una cuerda de una yarda de longitud.

2 Cada compañero estima cuán largo es el objeto en yardas y anota su estimación en su hoja de anotaciones. (Las estimaciones de los compañeros no tienen que coincidir).

3 Los compañeros se ayudan entre sí para medir el objeto a la yarda entera más próxima, usando la cuerda de una yarda de longitud.

4 Los compañeros repiten cada uno de los pasos anteriores hasta que hayan completado sus hojas de anotaciones.

Unit 4 Module 2 | Session 2 *class set, plus more as needed, stored in the Work Place bin*

NOMBRE Xavier _____ |FECHA _____

4B Medir en yardas — Hoja de anotaciones

Usa tu cuerda de yarda para estimar y medir la longitud en yardas.

- Elige lo que desees medir. Escríbelo en tu hoja de anotaciones.
- Registra tu estimación. ¿Cuántas yardas de largo crees que tiene? Haz esto antes de medir.
- Mide la longitud a la yarda más cercana usando la cuerda de yarda.

Mi objeto	Mi estimación	Longitud real
a La altura del Sr. Frisby	___2___ yardas	___2___ yardas
b	_____ yardas	_____ yardas
c	_____ yardas	_____ yardas
d	_____ yardas	_____ yardas
e	_____ yardas	_____ yardas
f	_____ yardas	_____ yardas

Bridges in Mathematics Grade 2 Teacher Masters — T3 — © The Math Learning Center | mathlearningcenter.org

---

Work Place Guide 4B Measuring in Yards

Summary

Students work in pairs to choose objects in and near the classroom to measure in yards. First, they find an object to measure and write the name of the object on their record sheets. Then they estimate the length of the object, and finally measure it to the nearest yard, using a yard-long piece of string.

Skills & Concepts

- Measure the length of an object in yards (2.MD.1)
- Estimate length in yards (2.MD.3)
- Measure length to the nearest whole unit in customary units (supports 2.MD)

Materials

Copies	Kit Materials	Classroom Materials
TM T1 Work Place Guide 4B Measuring in Yards **TM T2** Work Place Instructions 4B Measuring in Yards **TM T3** 4B Measuring in Yards Record Sheet		• 1-yard lengths of heavy cotton string (3)

Assessment & Differentiation

Here are some quick observational assessments you can make as students begin to play this game on their own. Use the results to differentiate as needed.

If you see that...	Differentiate	Example
Students are having trouble measuring lengths longer than a yard with the string.	**SUPPORT** Remind students of the measuring techniques discussed in class.	Students can work together to stretch out the string, hold it down on one end, and then move the other end around to measure a second yard.
Students are having a hard time finding appropriate items to measure.	**SUPPORT** Show students how to measure one appropriate item in the room and then challenge them to find other objects around the room that are similar in length, or longer than, the first object. You might also have an adult helper take small groups of students to locations around the school that might have objects suitable for measuring in yards, such as the gym, the cafeteria, and/or the playground.	Have students estimate and measure the height of the classroom door, and then find other objects around the room that are at least as long as the door is high.
Students are having a hard time measuring to the nearest whole yard.	**SUPPORT** If this problem comes up during Work Places, you may want to discuss it with the entire class. First, solicit and try suggestions from the students. Then if it doesn't come from the class, show students how to fold a yard-string in half and mark it at the half-way point with a small piece of masking tape. Then show them that when an object doesn't measure an exact number of whole yards, they can look to see whether the "final bit" falls before the half-way mark, exactly at the half-way mark, or after the half-way mark.	If an object measures 3 yards and some more, look to see if the "some more" is less than half, exactly half, or more than half a yard. If it is less than a half, it is 3 yards if measured to the nearest yard. If it is more than a half, it is 4 yards if measured to the nearest yard. If it falls exactly at the half-way mark, students can be encouraged to record 3 ½, or 3 and a half.
One or more students are working quickly and successfully to complete the sheet.	**CHALLENGE** Have students find pairs of objects for each line of the sheet. The pairs of objects should be as close to the same length as possible.	Clever students may list "left side of the door" and "right side of the door" as a potential pair.

Instrucciones de Work Place 4B Medir en yardas

1   Cada estudiante necesita una hoja de anotaciones y un lápiz. Las parejas de estudiantes comparten una cuerda de una yarda de longitud.

2   Cada compañero estima cuán largo es el objeto en yardas y anota su estimación en su hoja de anotaciones. (Las estimaciones de los compañeros no tienen que coincidir).

3   Los compañeros se ayudan entre sí para medir el objeto a la yarda entera más próxima, usando la cuerda de una yarda de longitud.

4   Los compañeros repiten cada uno de los pasos anteriores hasta que hayan completado sus hojas de anotaciones.

Unit 4 Module 2 | Session 2 *class set, plus more as needed, stored in the Work Place bin*

NOMBRE Xavier | FECHA

4B Medir en yardas — Hoja de anotaciones

Usa tu cuerda de yarda para estimar y medir la longitud en yardas.

- Elige lo que desees medir. Escríbelo en tu hoja de anotaciones.
- Registra tu estimación. ¿Cuántas yardas de largo crees que tiene? Haz esto antes de medir.
- Mide la longitud a la yarda más cercana usando la cuerda de yarda.

Mi objeto	Mi estimación	Longitud real
a La altura del Sr. Frisby	2 yardas	2 yardas
b	_____ yardas	_____ yardas
c	_____ yardas	_____ yardas
d	_____ yardas	_____ yardas
e	_____ yardas	_____ yardas
f	_____ yardas	_____ yardas

Bridges in Mathematics Grade 2 Teacher Masters   **T3**   © The Math Learning Center | mathlearningcenter.org

Work Place Guide 4B Measuring in Yards

Summary

Students work in pairs to choose objects in and near the classroom to measure in yards. First, they find an object to measure and write the name of the object on their record sheets. Then they estimate the length of the object, and finally measure it to the nearest yard, using a yard-long piece of string.

Skills & Concepts

- Measure the length of an object in yards (2.MD.1)
- Estimate length in yards (2.MD.3)
- Measure length to the nearest whole unit in customary units (supports 2.MD)

Materials

Copies	Kit Materials	Classroom Materials
TM T1 Work Place Guide 4B Measuring in Yards **TM T2** Work Place Instructions 4B Measuring in Yards **TM T3** 4B Measuring in Yards Record Sheet		· 1-yard lengths of heavy cotton string (3)

Assessment & Differentiation

Here are some quick observational assessments you can make as students begin to play this game on their own. Use the results to differentiate as needed.

If you see that...	Differentiate	Example
Students are having trouble measuring lengths longer than a yard with the string.	**SUPPORT** Remind students of the measuring techniques discussed in class.	Students can work together to stretch out the string, hold it down on one end, and then move the other end around to measure a second yard.
Students are having a hard time finding appropriate items to measure.	**SUPPORT** Show students how to measure one appropriate item in the room and then challenge them to find other objects around the room that are similar in length, or longer than, the first object. You might also have an adult helper take small groups of students to locations around the school that might have objects suitable for measuring in yards, such as the gym, the cafeteria, and/or the playground.	Have students estimate and measure the height of the classroom door, and then find other objects around the room that are at least as long as the door is high.
Students are having a hard time measuring to the nearest whole yard.	**SUPPORT** If this problem comes up during Work Places, you may want to discuss it with the entire class. First, solicit and try suggestions from the students. Then if it doesn't come from the class, show students how to fold a yard-string in half and mark it at the half-way point with a small piece of masking tape. Then show them that when an object doesn't measure an exact number of whole yards, they can look to see whether the "final bit" falls before the half-way mark, exactly at the half-way mark, or after the half-way mark.	If an object measures 3 yards and some more, look to see if the "some more" is less than half, exactly half, or more than half a yard. If it is less than a half, it is 3 yards if measured to the nearest yard. If it is more than a half, it is 4 yards if measured to the nearest yard. If it falls exactly at the half-way mark, students can be encouraged to record 3 ½, or 3 and a half.
One or more students are working quickly and successfully to complete the sheet.	**CHALLENGE** Have students find pairs of objects for each line of the sheet. The pairs of objects should be as close to the same length as possible.	Clever students may list "left side of the door" and "right side of the door" as a potential pair.

Instrucciones de Work Place 4B Medir en yardas

1   Cada estudiante necesita una hoja de anotaciones y un lápiz. Las parejas de estudiantes comparten una cuerda de una yarda de longitud.

2   Cada compañero estima cuán largo es el objeto en yardas y anota su estimación en su hoja de anotaciones. (Las estimaciones de los compañeros no tienen que coincidir).

3   Los compañeros se ayudan entre sí para medir el objeto a la yarda entera más próxima, usando la cuerda de una yarda de longitud.

4   Los compañeros repiten cada uno de los pasos anteriores hasta que hayan completado sus hojas de anotaciones.

Unit 4 Module 2 | Session 2 *class set, plus more as needed, stored in the Work Place bin*

NOMBRE Xavier _____ | FECHA _____

4B Medir en yardas — Hoja de anotaciones

Usa tu cuerda de yarda para estimar y medir la longitud en yardas.

- Elige lo que desees medir. Escríbelo en tu hoja de anotaciones.
- Registra tu estimación. ¿Cuántas yardas de largo crees que tiene? Haz esto antes de medir.
- Mide la longitud a la yarda más cercana usando la cuerda de yarda.

Mi objeto	Mi estimación	Longitud real
a La altura del Sr. Frisby	___2___ yardas	___2___ yardas
b	_____ yardas	_____ yardas
c	_____ yardas	_____ yardas
d	_____ yardas	_____ yardas
e	_____ yardas	_____ yardas
f	_____ yardas	_____ yardas